# EXTRAORDINARY (CERAPODA) DINOSAURS

## CLASSIFY THE FEATURES OF PREHISTORIC CREATURES

DINO SORTED!

DISCARDED

SONYA NEWLAND

W

First published in Great Britain in 2021 by
The Watts Publishing Group
Copyright © The Watts Publishing Group, 2021

 Produced for Franklin Watts by
White-Thomson Publishing Ltd
www.wtpub.co.uk

HB ISBN 978 1 4451 7356 6
PB ISBN 978 1 4451 7357 3

Credits
Editor: Sonya Newland
Designer: Dan Prescott, Couper Street Type Co.

The publisher would like to thank the following for permission to reproduce their pictures:
Alamy: Stocktrek Images, Inc. 6, 19b, 30, Alberto Paredes 11t, Friedrich Saurer 27t; Getty Images: Peter Bull 15b; Shutterstock: Herschel Hoffmeyer cover, 8–9, 19t, 28–29, Warpaint 4, 5l, 12–13, 15t, 16–17, 24–25, 26, Catmando 5r, 10, 11b, Denis Simonov 5b, YuRi Photolife 7, 22, Elenarts 9, 13, Michael Rosskothen 14, Daniel Eskridge 17b, 20–21, 25, Philippe Clement 17t, Ralf Juergen Kraft 18, AKKHARAT JARUSILAWONG 21, David Herraez Calzada 23t, Jean-Michel Girard 23b, Matis75 27b.

All design elements from Shutterstock.

Printed in China

Franklin Watts
An imprint of
Hachette Children's Group
Part of The Watts Publishing Group
Carmelite House
50 Victoria Embankment
London EC4Y 0DZ

An Hachette UK Company
www.hachette.co.uk
www.franklinwatts.co.uk

## PRONUNCIATION GUIDE

*Albertaceratops* (al-berta-SERRA-tops)

*Camptosaurus* (KAMP-toe-SORE-us)

*Centrosaurus* (sen-troh-SORE-us)

*Chasmosaurus* (KAZ-mo-sore-us)

*Dracorex* (DRAY-koh-reks)

*Edmontosaurus* (ed-MON-toe-sore-rus)

*Heterodontosaurus* (HET-er-oh-DONT-oh-sore-us)

*Hypsilophodon* (hip-sih-LOH-foh-don)

*Iguanodon* (ig-WAH-no-don)

*Lambeosaurus* (lam-BEE-oh-SORE-us)

*Leptoceratops* (lep-toe-KER-ah-tops)

*Lesothosaurus* (le-SO-toe-SORE-us)

*Micropachycephalosaurus* (mike-row-pak-i-KEF-al-oh-SORE-us)

*Ouranosaurus* (oo-RAH-noh-SORE-us)

*Pachycephalosaurus* (pak-i-KEF-al-oh-SORE-us)

*Pachyrhinosaurus* (pack-ee-RINE-oh-SORE-us)

*Parasaurolophus* (pa-ra-sore-ROL-of-us)

*Psittacosaurus* (SIT-ak-oh-SORE-us)

*Saurolophus* (SORE-oh-LOAF-us)

*Shantungosaurus* (shan-TUN-go-sore-us)

*Stegoceras* (ste-GO-ser-as)

*Tianyulong* (te-AN-yoo-long)

*Torosaurus* (tor-oh-SORE-us)

*Triceratops* (tri-SERRA-tops)

# CONTENTS

# MEET THE

DINOSAURS ARE DIVIDED INTO CATEGORIES THAT SHARE CERTAIN FEATURES. THE CERAPODA BELONG TO A CATEGORY CALLED ORNITHISCHIA, OR 'BIRD-HIPPED' DINOSAURS. THE CERAPODA THEMSELVES ARE SPLIT INTO TWO MAIN GROUPS — THE ORNITHOPODA AND THE MARGINOCEPHALIA.

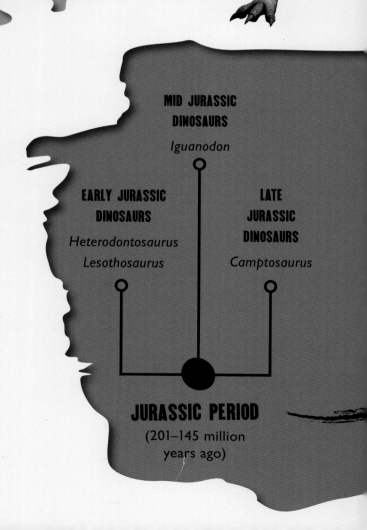

*Camptosaurus*

Ornithopods ('bird-feet') were common from the Late Triassic Period. They were one of the most successful and long-lasting groups of dinosaurs. Within this group were several smaller families of dinosaurs, including heterodontosaurids, hypsilophodontids, iguanodontids and hadrosaurids. Ornithopods usually walked on two legs, but some may have moved on all fours when grazing.

The Marginocephalia ('fringed heads') emerged in the Jurassic Period and became more common throughout the Cretaceous Period. The two main groups were Pachycephalosauria, characterised by their thick skulls, and Ceratopsia, which had horns.

**MID JURASSIC DINOSAURS**

*Iguanodon*

**EARLY JURASSIC DINOSAURS**

*Heterodontosaurus*
*Lesothosaurus*

**LATE JURASSIC DINOSAURS**

*Camptosaurus*

## JURASSIC PERIOD
(201–145 million years ago)

# CERAPODA

Psittacosaurus

Centrosaurus

The Cerapoda were wiped out 66 million years ago in a mass extinction event that destroyed three-quarters of all life on Earth. Scientists believe that a huge asteroid crashed into Earth in the area that is now Mexico. The asteroid impact filled the air with deadly gas and dust for many years. This changed the climate so dramatically that few living things could survive.

**EARLY CRETACEOUS DINOSAURS**

*Hypsilophodon*
*Ouranosaurus*
*Psittacosaurus*

**LATE CRETACEOUS DINOSAURS**

*Centrosaurus*
*Lambeosaurus*
*Parasaurolophus*
*Shantungosaurus*
*Torosaurus*
*Triceratops*

**CRETACEOUS PERIOD**
(145–66 million years ago)

# LITTLE AND LARGE

THE ORNITHOPODS OF THE EARLY JURASSIC PERIOD WERE QUITE SMALL ANIMALS. OVER TIME, SOME GROUPS EVOLVED TO BECOME MUCH LARGER. BUT THROUGHOUT ALL THEIR TIME ON EARTH, THE CERAPODA CAME IN MANY DIFFERENT SIZES.

▼ Although only about 1.75 m long, Heterodontosaurus was one of the largest of the heterodontosaurids.

Some of the earliest heterodontosaurids, such as the tiny *Tianyulong*, were only about 75 cm from beak to tail tip – no larger than a dog! The hypsilophodontids were a bit bigger, reaching up to 3 m. The iguanodotids were much bigger, perhaps up to 9 m. The hadrosaurids of the Late Cretaceous Period were the largest of all. Some grew to 15 m!

The early Ornithopods were small and light, which meant they could move quickly. They were bipeds – able to run on two legs. As they grew bigger, their weight became cumbersome, and many later species walked on four legs.

The Marginocephalia may have evolved from the Ornithopods. They generally had bigger, more barrel-like bodies than their early relatives. However, they still came in a wide range of sizes, from the 1-m *Micropachycephalosaurus* to species of Ceratopsia that could be more than 9 m long.

◀ Members of the ceratopsid group ranged from 1 m to more than 9 m long. *Pachyrhinosaurus* could be up to 8 m.

It's hard to say exactly how big or small different Cerapoda were. For some species, only a few bones have been found, so palaeontologists have to estimate the sizes. As new fossils are found, experts may identify bigger or smaller species.

# SORTED:

## SHANTUNGOSAURUS

SHANTUNGOSAURUS LIVED IN WHAT IS NOW CHINA IN THE LATE CRETACEOUS PERIOD. SEVERAL MASSIVE DINOSAURS LIVED IN ASIA AT THIS TIME, BUT SHANTUNGOSAURUS WAS A MATCH FOR THEM ALL!

## ↖ BIG HEAD

*Shantungosaurs* had a long head. The largest skull found measures 1.63 m! At the end of its skull, *Shantungosaurus* had a bony beak. In its long jaws were 1,500 tiny, sharp teeth, which it used for slicing and chewing plant matter.

## HUGE HADROSAUR

The hadrosaurids were the largest type of Cerapoda, but *Shantungosaurus* was the biggest of them all. Although palaeontologists have not found a full skeleton, they have worked out its size from its leg bones. One thigh bone measured 1.7 m – that's about as big as a bicycle!

## TAIL

*Shantungosaurus* had a thick, powerful tail, which was carried stiffly above the ground. The heavy tail probably helped to balance the dinosaur as it walked.

## GETTING AROUND

Like most of the bigger Ornithopods, *Shantungosaurus* walked on four legs almost all the time. However, despite being big and heavy, it may also have been able to lift up its front legs and run on its back ones.

## DINOMIGHTY!

*Shantungosaurus* may have been the biggest dinosaur ever to have existed outside the group of giant sauropods.

# SPECIALISED LEGS AND FEET

THE CERAPODA WERE A MIXED GROUP. SOME WERE BIPEDS, WALKING ON TWO LEGS. OTHERS WERE QUADRUPEDS, MOVING ON ALL FOURS. THE LEGS AND FEET OF EACH SPECIES WERE ADAPTED TO THEIR SIZE, WEIGHT AND ENVIRONMENT.

The small, light heterodontosaurids and hypsilophodontids walked upright on two legs. Their arms were short, with five-fingered hands that may have been used for digging up plant roots. They had long, slim back legs. Some early Ornithopods had four toes, but most later species only had three.

◄ *Hypsilophodon* was small and light. It used its long, strong back legs to run at up to 40 kph.

Most baby hadrosaurids walked on two legs, but the large adults probably moved more easily on four. They had wide, short toes and fleshy pads on their feet, similar to the gigantic sauropods.

Evidence suggests that early iguanodontids moved on both two legs and four. They had unusual feet, with close, hoof-like second, third and fourth toes. Some experts think that these toes may have been fused together with skin.

◀ Footprints, such as these three-toed Ornithopod tracks, can tell us a lot about this group of dinosaurs. For example, the distance between the footprints can suggest the size and speed of the dinosaur.

◀ Like the early Ornithopods, the medium-sized Pachycephalosauria, such as *Stegoceras*, had wide hips, long back legs and short front limbs.

One difference between the two groups of Marginocephalia dinosaurs was in the way they walked. The Pachycephalosauria were bipeds. They had strong back legs and much smaller front ones, which were more like arms. Early Ceratopsia had a similar body shape, but later species, such as *Triceratops*, were quadrupeds, with four thick, strong legs.

# SORTED:

## IGUANODON

IGUANODON WAS THE BIGGEST TYPE OF IGUANODONTID. AT ABOUT 10 M, IT WAS TWICE AS LONG AS THE LARGEST REPTILE ALIVE TODAY, THE SALTWATER CROCODILE!

### QUICK FACTS

**PERIOD:**
Early Cretaceous

**LIVED IN:**
Europe, North Africa, North America

**LENGTH:**
10 m

**WEIGHT:**
4,000 kg

### DINOMIGHTY!

*Iguanodon* was only the second dinosaur ever to be discovered, in around 1820. When experts first examined the teeth, they thought they must be from a rhinoceros or a fish!

## SLOW AND FAST

Like most other iguanodontids, *Iguanodon* could move on either two legs or four. It probably spent most of its time grazing on four legs, slicing leaves from trees and plants with its strong beak. Up on its hind legs, it could move at around 20 kph.

## UNUSUAL HANDS

The bones in *Iguanodon*'s wrists were fused together. It had five fingers on each hand. The three middle fingers were close together, forming blunt claws, like a hoof. The outer finger was separate from the others and stuck out sideways.

## USEFUL DIGITS

This outer finger was prehensile. That means it could be moved in a way that allowed it to wrap around things. This probably helped *Iguanodon* grab and hold plants. *Iguanodon*'s inner finger had a cone-shaped thumb spike, which may have been used as a weapon.

# BEAKS AND TEETH

MOST CERAPODA HAD A TOOTHLESS, BONY BEAK AT THE FRONT OF THEIR SKULL. SOME HAD SHARP, NARROW BEAKS THAT WERE GOOD FOR BITING TOUGH PLANTS. OTHERS HAD WIDE, FLAT BILLS LIKE MODERN DUCKS. THE CERAPODA ALSO HAD MANY DIFFERENT SIZES AND SHAPES OF TEETH.

The Ornithopods were a bit like cows and deer today. They grazed on plants that grew close to the ground. The beaks that first developed in the heterodontosaurids helped them dig up roots and other vegetation.

▲ Ceratopsids like *Albertaceratops* developed with a hooked beak and rows of teeth at the back of the mouth for shearing plants.

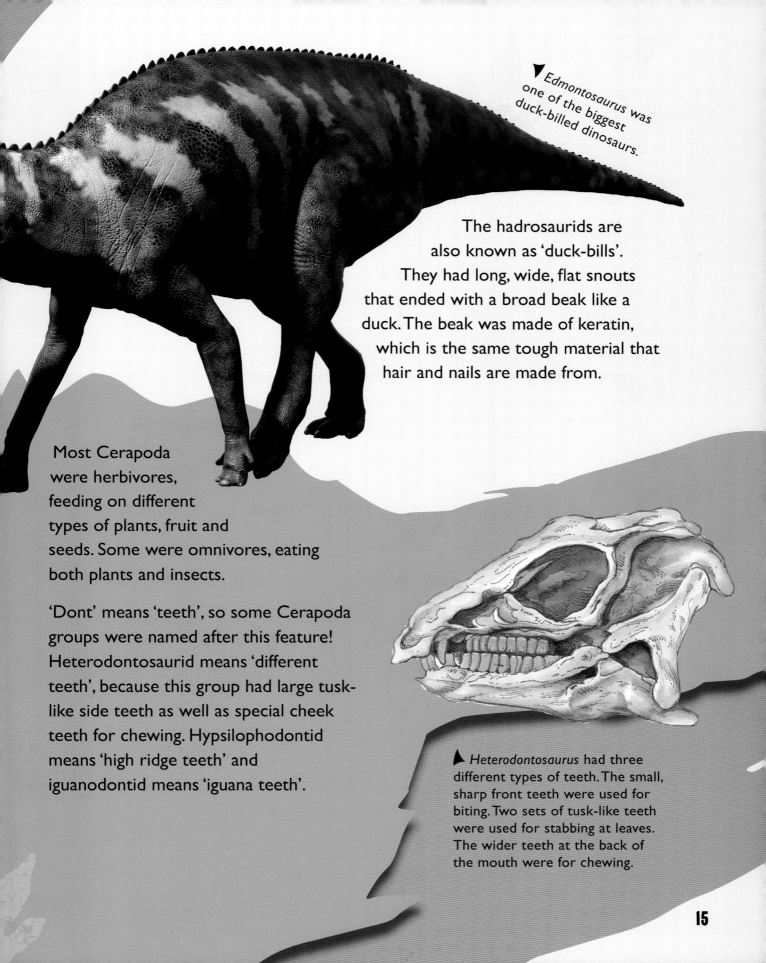

▼ Edmontosaurus was one of the biggest duck-billed dinosaurs.

The hadrosaurids are also known as 'duck-bills'. They had long, wide, flat snouts that ended with a broad beak like a duck. The beak was made of keratin, which is the same tough material that hair and nails are made from.

Most Cerapoda were herbivores, feeding on different types of plants, fruit and seeds. Some were omnivores, eating both plants and insects.

'Dont' means 'teeth', so some Cerapoda groups were named after this feature! Heterodontosaurid means 'different teeth', because this group had large tusk-like side teeth as well as special cheek teeth for chewing. Hypsilophodontid means 'high ridge teeth' and iguanodontid means 'iguana teeth'.

▲ Heterodontosaurus had three different types of teeth. The small, sharp front teeth were used for biting. Two sets of tusk-like teeth were used for stabbing at leaves. The wider teeth at the back of the mouth were for chewing.

# SORTED:

# PARASAUROLOPHUS

THE LARGE HERBIVOROUS HADROSAURID PARASAUROPHOLUS LIVED IN WHAT IS NOW THE USA AND CANADA. IT SPENT ITS LIFE GRAZING ON LEAVES, TWIGS AND PINE NEEDLES.

## QUICK FACTS

**PERIOD:**
Late Cretaceous

**LIVED IN:**
North America

**LENGTH:**
11 m

**WEIGHT:**
3,500 kg

## DINOMIGHTY!

*Parasaurolophus*'s crest could probably emit very loud sounds over long distances, in the same way that whales and elephants communicate.

# BROAD BEAK

*Parasaurolophus*'s skull ended in a narrow, flat beak with a sharp edge. This was good for shearing off and gathering up mouthfuls of tough plant matter.

# HEAD CREST

*Parasaurolophus*'s most famous feature is its long, bony head crest. The crest extended from the top of the head and was as long as the skull itself. Some experts think it may have been used like an instrument to call out to other members of the herd. Others suggest it was a way of getting rid of body heat, similar to the way an elephant's ears carry heat away from its body.

# TOUGH TEETH

Its jaws were packed with hundreds of small teeth, but only a few were used at a time. As *Parasaurolophus*'s front teeth wore away and fell out, the back teeth gradually shifted forward to take their place. The teeth were used to grind up plants in the mouth before swallowing.

# BONY HEADS

PALAEONTOLOGISTS HAVEN'T FOUND MANY PACHYCEPHALOSAURIA BONES, SO WE DON'T KNOW TOO MUCH ABOUT THEM WHEN COMPARED TO SOME OTHER DINOSAUR GROUPS. ONE THING WE DO KNOW, HOWEVER, IS THAT THE PACHYCEPHALOSAURS STOOD OUT FROM THE OTHER CERAPODA BECAUSE OF THEIR DISTINCTIVE THICK SKULLS.

In some species, the skull was shaped like a dome and was quite noticeable. But the skull could also be flat or wedge-shaped. In species such as *Stegoceras*, young dinosaurs had a thick, flat skull that got more domed as they became adults.

▶ *Dracorex* (named after a character in the Harry Potter books) had a thick but flat skull. Some palaeontologists think it may actually be a young *Pachycephalosaurus*.

The domes were often surrounded by bony lumps, like blunt horns. In many dinosaurs, bumps and spikes are arranged in patterns, but in the Pachycephalosauria they appear to be randomly positioned on the head.

◄ Some palaeontologists now think that Pachycephalosauria fought by 'flank-butting' – using their heads to hit each other on the side of the body.

Experts have different ideas about why the Pachycephalosauria developed these thick skulls. Some think the dinosaurs head-butted each other in fights, so they evolved with a thick dome to protect the brain. Others suggest that the domes may have been a way for the Pachycephalosauria to recognise others of their own species.

◄ The domes may also have been used for display. If this is the case, then they may have been brightly coloured.

# SORTED:

# PACHYCEPHALOSAURUS

THE BIGGEST OF THE BONE-HEADED DINOSAURS, *PACHYCEPHALOSAURUS* IS FAMOUS FOR ITS HUGE DOMED SKULL. THIS FEATURE MIGHT HAVE PROTECTED THE DINOSAUR'S TINY BRAIN!

## SKULL AND DOME

The dome that formed part of *Pachycephalosaurus*'s skull may not have been solid bone. Instead, it may have been softer inside, with holes in it like a sponge. This would have reduced the weight of the skull – but it would also have reduced its strength, making head-butting riskier.

## BIG EYES

Fossil remains of *Pachycephalosaurus* show that this dinosaur had large eye sockets that faced forward in the skull. The size suggests that *Pachycephalosaurus* had big eyes and good eyesight compared to some dinosaurs. The fact that the eyes faced forward means that this dinosaur probably had binocular vision – that is, it could focus on an object with both eyes.

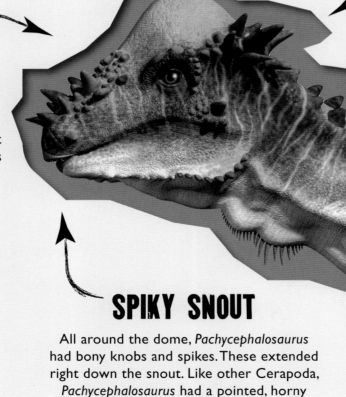

## SPIKY SNOUT

All around the dome, *Pachycephalosaurus* had bony knobs and spikes. These extended right down the snout. Like other Cerapoda, *Pachycephalosaurus* had a pointed, horny beak at the end of its snout.

**PERIOD:**
Late Cretaceous

**LIVED IN:**
North America

**LENGTH:**
8 m

**WEIGHT:**
3,000 kg

# DINOMIGHTY!

The dome of bone on *Pachycephalosaurus*'s head could be 25 cm thick. That's about 20 times thicker than the skulls of most dinosaurs!

# NECK FRILLS

OF ALL THE TYPES OF CERAPODA, ONE GROUP HAD A PARTICULARLY DISTINCTIVE FEATURE. THE CERATOPSIA ARE FAMOUS FOR THEIR NECK FRILLS. THESE RANGED FROM VERY SMALL, BONY FRAMES IN EARLY DINOSAURS LIKE *LEPTOCERATOPS* TO THE GIGANTIC FRILLS ON *TOROSAURUS.*

The frill was not a separate part of the skeleton. It was an extension of the bones in the neck. The frills came in all different shapes and sizes, and some had bony lumps or horns around the edge. The bone of the frill was covered in tough skin.

▼ *Chasmosaurus* was a medium-sized ceratopsid, but its neck frill was very long. It was broader at the ends than the front.

The covering of skin made the frills look solid. In fact, most frills had big holes in them, like windows in a frame. Bone is heavy, so having these holes reduced the weight of the frill.

▼ *Triceratops* had an unusual neck frill, which was made of solid bone instead of having holes in the middle like the frills of most ceratopsids.

Palaeontologists originally thought that necks frills were a form of protection – to defend against carnivores trying to take a bite. But neck frills were made of quite thin bone and had holes in them, so they would have broken under attack. Instead, the frill was probably used for display. The skin may have been brightly coloured to help attract a mate.

► As well as their frills, many ceratopsids had horns on their nose and above their eyes, like *Triceratops* (see page 27).

# SORTED:

# TOROSAURUS

TOROSAURUS WAS ONE OF THE BIGGEST CERATOPSIDS. ITS NAME MEANS 'PERFORATED LIZARD'. THINGS THAT ARE PERFORATED HAVE HOLES IN THEM, AND THIS DINOSAUR GOT ITS NAME BECAUSE OF THE HOLES IN ITS HUGE NECK FRILL.

## A GROWN-UP *TRICERATOPS*?

Some palaeontologists think that *Torosaurus* may be the fully grown version of *Triceratops*. Others argue that they must be two different species, and use the neck frill as evidence. Even on the youngest *Torosauruses* discovered, the neck frill is bigger than *Triceratops*.

## BIG FRILL

The huge fan-shaped neck frill stretched out from low on the back of *Torosaurus*'s skull. The frill was thinner than in some other species, such as *Triceratops*. This was probably to reduce the weight, as the frill was so large.

**QUICK FACTS**

**PERIOD:**
Late Cretaceous

**LIVED IN:**
North America

**LENGTH:**
7.5 m

**WEIGHT:**
4,000–6,000 kg

## HORNS

Behind the frill, *Torosaurus* had several pairs of small horns. It had two eye horns, like other ceratopsids, but its nose horn was shorter than in other dinosaurs.

## DINOMIGHTY!

*Torosaurus* had one of the biggest skulls of any creature ever to have walked the Earth. With its huge frill, the skull was a massive 2.8 m long – that's about as long as you and a friend lying head to head!

## BIG HEAD

Most ceratopsids had big heads – about one-fifth of their body size – but *Torosaurus*'s head was even bigger. The skull of this Cerapoda made up one-third of its body length!

# EXTRAORDINARY FEATURES

WITH THEIR BEAKS, DOMED HEADS OR FRILLS, ALL THE SUB-GROUPS OF THE CERAPODA HAD THEIR OWN UNIQUE LOOK. BUT THESE WEREN'T THE ONLY EXTRAORDINARY FEATURES THIS CATEGORY OF DINOSAURS HAD.

▲ *Lambeosaurus* had a strangely shaped hollow crest on its head.

Some of the hadrosaurids had amazing head crests. These curved, bony tubes could sometimes be as long as the skull itself. The crest was covered in skin and there may also have been a web of skin between the crest and the neck.

A few Cerapoda, such as *Saurolophus*, had unusual spikes on their heads. This was especially strange in the hadrosaurid *Lambeosaurus*. This dinosaur had a spiky projection sticking out of its crest, giving the crest the shape of an axe!

*Psittacosaurus* was an early type of Ceratopsian. A fossil of this dinosaur was discovered that had an unusual tail feature – long bristles, or 'filaments'. No one knows the purpose of these long, tube-like structures, but some experts think they may have been used to attract a mate.

◀ *Psittacosaurus* was covered in tiny scales.

The ceratopsids often had three horns – two above their eyes and one above the beak. They either had long eye horns and a short nose horn or vice versa. Males probably used them to fight predators and each other.

◀ The horns on *Triceratops* could be up to 1 m long.

# SORTED:

## OURANOSAURUS

THIS EARLY CRETACEOUS DINOSAUR HAS PUZZLED SOME EXPERTS BECAUSE OF ITS UNUSUAL FEATURES. AT FIRST IT WAS CLASSIFIED AS AN IGUANADONTID, BUT NOW PALAEONTOGOSISTS THINK IT MAY HAVE BEEN AN EARLY HADROSAURID.

## QUICK FACTS

**PERIOD:**
Early Cretaceous

**LIVED IN:**
West Africa

**LENGTH:**
7 m

**WEIGHT:**
2,200–4,000 kg

## UNUSUAL HEAD

*Ouranosaurus*'s head was bigger and its jaws longer than most iguanodontids. Along the top of its snout, above the eyes, were two wide bumps. These may have served the same purpose as the small horns on modern antelopes, which are used for display.

## SAIL

Even more unusual is that *Ouranosaurus* has a 'sail' on its back. This was a row of spines along the backbone, whch were covered with skin. The sail may have been brightly coloured to act as a warning to predators. *Ouranosaurus* is the only member of the Cerapoda to have this feature.

## AN ORDINARY ORNITHOPOD?

In many ways *Ouranosaurus* was similar to others of its type. It was powerfully built, with long, strong back legs and smaller – but still strong – front legs. It had hoof-like hands and feet, and a thumb-spike like the iguanodontids.

## DINOMIGHTY!

*Ouranosaurus* had unusually high nostrils. These may have come in handy when grazing in low, muddy areas, allowing it to crop the plants without getting mud up its nose!

# GLOSSARY

**ASTEROID** – a large rock that forms in space and orbits the Sun

**BIPEDS** – animals that walk on their two back legs

**CARNIVORE** – an animal that eats meat

**CREST** – a feature on the top of the head, made of bone, feathers, fur or skin

**EVOLVE** – to change and develop gradually over time

**FILAMENTS** – very thin strands, like threads

**FOSSIL** – the shape of a plant or animal that has been preserved in rock for a very long time

**FUSED** – joined together

**GRAZING** – feeding slowly on low-lying vegetation

**HERBIVORE** – an animal that eats only plants and fruit

**KERATIN** – a fibre-like substance that hair, nails, claws, horns, etc. are made from

**MASS EXTINCTION** – the death of many living things, when species stop existing completely

**MATE** – a reproductive partner

**OMNIVORE** – an animal that eats both plants and meat

**ORNITHISCHIA** – 'bird-hipped' dinosaurs, one of the two main groups of dinosaurs

**PALAEONTOLOGIST** – a scientist who studies dinosaurs and prehistoric life

**PREDATOR** – an animal that hunts and kills other animals for food

**PREHENSILE** – describing things that can move in a way that allows them to grasp objects

**QUADRUPED** – describing an animal that walks on four legs rather than two

**SKULL** – the bones that make up the head and face

**SPECIES** – a group of living things that are closely related and share similar features

**SUB-GROUP** – a group of animals within a larger category that have particular features in common

**UNIQUE** – not the same as anything else

# FURTHER INFORMATION

## BOOKS

*The Age of Dinosaurs* (Dinosaur Infosaurus)
by Katie Woolley (Wayland, 2018)

*Birth of the Dinosaurs* (Planet Earth)
by Michael Bright (Wayland, 2016)

*Triceratops and other Horned Herbivores* (Dinosaurs!)
by David West (Franklin Watts, 2015)

*Parasaurolophus and other Beaked Herbivores* (Dinosaurs!)
by David West (Franklin Watts, 2015)

## DRAW YOUR OWN

Use the information in this book to design a new Cerapoda. Remember to include the features of whatever sub-group you choose. Then give your dinosaur a name.

## WEBSITES

www.amnh.org/exhibitions/dinosaurs-ancient-fossils/display-or-defense/my-what-a-big-skull-you-have
www.amnh.org/exhibitions/dinosaurs-ancient-fossils/display-or-defense/the-horned-dinosaurs
Get to know the Ceratopsians with these articles from the American Museum of Natural History.

www.bbc.co.uk/programmes/p00b9cw3
Watch *Iguanodons* on the move in this video clip from the BBC's series *Walking with Dinosaurs*.

www.nationalgeographic.com/animals/prehistoric/triceratops-horridus/
www.nationalgeographic.com/animals/prehistoric/pachycephalosaurus-wyomingensis/
Find out about *Triceratops* and *Pachycephalosaurus* in these fact files from National Geographic, and search for other Cerapoda.

The website addresses (URLs) included in this book were valid at the time of going to press. However, it is possible that contents or addresses may have changed since the publication of this book. No responsibility for any such changes can be accepted by either the author or the publisher.

# INDEX